The MAILBOX®

Organize OCTOBER Now!™

grades K-1

Everything You Need for a Successful October

Monthly Organizing Tools
Manage your time, classroom, and students with monthly organizational tools.

Essential Skills Practice
Practice essential skills this month with engaging activities and reproducibles.

October in the Classroom
Carry your monthly themes into every corner of the classroom.

Ready-to-Go Learning Centers and Skills Practice
Bring October to life right now!

Managing Editor: Sharon Murphy

Editorial Team: Becky S. Andrews, Kimberley Bruck, Karen P. Shelton, Diane Badden, Thad H. McLaurin, Kimberly Brugger-Murphy, Cindy K. Daoust, Gerri Primak, Leanne Stratton, Karen A. Brudnak, Sarah Hamblet, Hope Rodgers, Dorothy C. McKinney, Randi Austin, Tracy Bowslaugh, Janet Boyce, Lisa Buchholz, Stacie Stone Davis, Margaret Elliott, Cynthia Holcomb, Angie Kutzer, Sabrina Lilly, Misty M. Slater, Valerie Wood Smith, Susan Walker, Tracey Wright

Production Team: Lisa K. Pitts, Pam Crane, Rebecca Saunders, Jennifer Tipton Cappoen, Chris Curry, Sarah Foreman, Theresa Lewis Goode, Clint Moore, Greg D. Rieves, Barry Slate, Donna K. Teal, Zane Williard, Tazmen Carlisle, Amy Kirtley-Hill, Cathy Edwards Simrell, Lynette Dickerson, Mark Rainey, Angela Kamstra, Sheila Krill

www.themailbox.com

Table of Contents

Monthly Organizing Tools

A collection of reproducible forms, notes, and other timesavers and organizational tools just for October

Medallion, Brag Tag, and Award 4
October Calendar 5
Center Checklist 6
Class List 7
Class Newsletters 8
Clip Art 10
Incentive Charts 11
Journal Cover 12
Monthly Planning Form 13
Open Page 14
Parent Reminder Note 15
School Notes 16
Family Fun 17

Essential Skills Practice

Fun, skill-building activities and reproducibles that combine the skills your students must learn with favorite October themes

Fall 18
Pumpkins 28
Spiders 36
Fire Safety 44

October in the Classroom

In a hurry to find a specific type of October activity? It's right here!

Arts & Crafts 50
Bulletin Boards & Displays 54
Centers 58
Games 62
Management Tips 66
Time Fillers 68
Writing Ideas & Prompts 70

Ready-to-Go Learning Centers and Skills Practice

Two center activities you can tear out and use almost instantly! Plus a collection of additional reproducible skill builders!

A Pumpkin Parade: number sequence (Learning Center) 74
Chew a Shoe: color words (Learning Center) 82
Additional October Reproducible Skill Builders 90

Skills Grid

	Fall	Pumpkins	Spiders	Fire Safety	Centers	Games	Time Fillers	Writing Ideas & Prompts	Learning Center: A Pumpkin Parade	Learning Center: Chew a Shoe	Ready-to-Go Skills Practice
Literacy											
visual discrimination						62					
rhyming pictures		28									
convey a message through pictures				45							
letter recognition	25										
uppercase and lowercase letters	20				58						
alphabetical order	21										
initial consonants: *b, m, s, w*											92
initial consonants: *f, g*	26										
initial consonant: *w*			43								
beginning sound /d/				46							
beginning sound /k/											90
beginning sound /s/			37								
onsets and rimes						59					
digraphs: *ch, sh, th*											93
color words			38							82, 89	91
sight words		31									
true or false		29									
reading repetitive text				44							
spelling						63					
early writing	18										
writing sentences	19										
journal prompts								70			
writing			36, 39								
descriptive writing		30						71			
informational writing								70			
creative writing								70, 71			
making a list							69				
telling a story							69				
Math											
counting to ten						62					
one-to-one correspondence				46							
number recognition	25										
identifying numerals			39								
number sequence		35							74, 81		
ordinal numbers		29									
comparing sets		30									94
even and odd numbers			38								
addition				45	59						
count by twos, fives, and tens	21										
subtraction											96
basic facts						63					
story problems			36								
shapes		34			58						
positional words	18										
nonstandard measurement	20										
order by length				49							
graphing	19										
tally marks		31									
patterns		28									
sorting by size			37								
sorting shapes											95
Science											
fire safety				44							

Medallion

Tape to the end of a student's pencil.

I've got good behavior WRAPPED UP!

TEC60976

Brag Tag

Use a child's words to finish the sentence starter.

I'm **BEAMING** because...

©The Mailbox® • *Organize October Now!*™ • TEC60976

Award

_____
student

is the PRIDE of the PATCH!

_____
teacher

_____
date

©The Mailbox® • *Organize October Now!*™ • TEC60976

Medallion, brag tag, and award: Copy onto colorful construction paper, cut out, and use as desired.

October

Sunday	Monday	Tuesday	Wednesday	Thursday	Friday	Saturday

Center Checklist

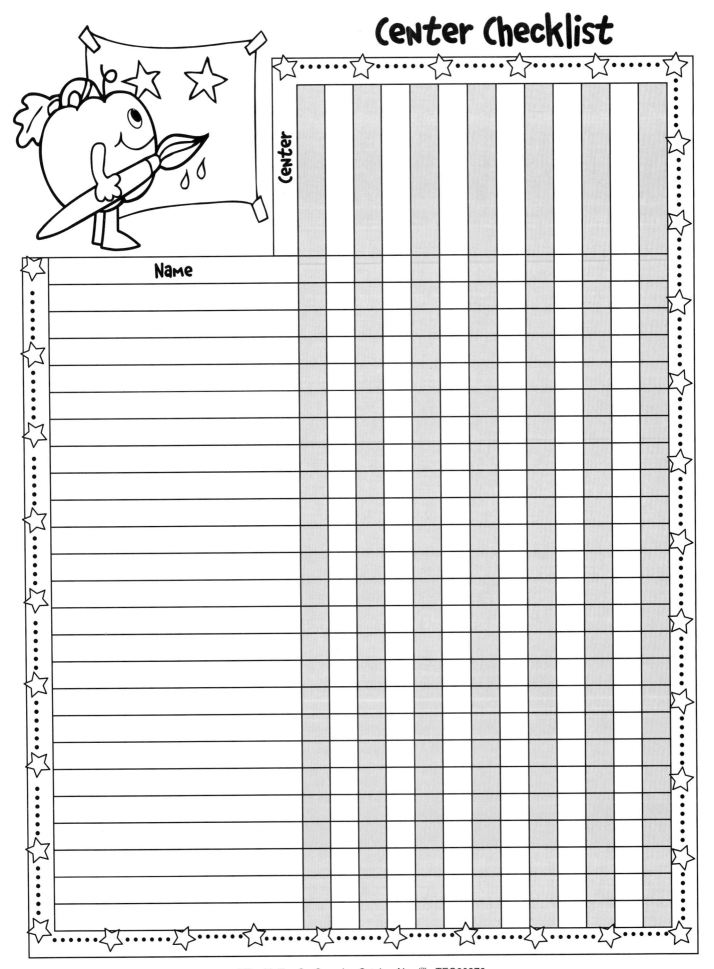

Center

Name

Class List

Name											

Classroom News

From _____

Date _____

Help Wanted

Special Thanks

Look What We Are Learning

☆ **Super Stars**

Please Remember

8

Classroom News

From _____

Date _____

9

TEC60976
TEC60976
TEC60976
TEC60976
TEC60976

©The Mailbox® • *Organize October Now!*™ • TEC60976

Clip art: Use the artwork on student papers and on correspondence such as announcements, forms, and parent notes.

Name _____

Date _____

You can do it!

Name _____

Date _____

···SWEET···SWEET···SWEET···SUCCESS!

Name _____

Date _____

Keep trying!

Incentive charts: Have students track their progress as they work toward a variety of goals.

My
Journal

Name

Journal cover: Make this page the front cover of your students' writing journals.

Materials to Collect:

Duties This Month:

Meetings:

To Do:

☆ ☆ ☆ ☆ ☆ ☆ ☆ ☆ ☆ ☆ ☆ ☆

Birthdays:

©The Mailbox® • *Organize October Now!*™ • TEC60976

Monthly planning form: Use this handy form to stay on top of each month's school-related responsibilities.

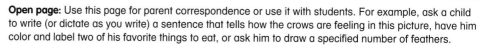

Open page: Use this page for parent correspondence or use it with students. For example, ask a child to write (or dictate as you write) a sentence that tells how the crows are feeling in this picture, have him color and label two of his favorite things to eat, or ask him to draw a specified number of feathers.

PLEASE REMEMBER:

date

Dear Parent,

Please remember

Thanks a lot!

©The Mailbox® • *Organize October Now!*™ • TEC60976

SCHOOL NOTE

SCHOOL NOTE

School notes: Use these notes for parent communications such as announcing an upcoming event, requesting supplies or volunteers, and writing messages of praise.

This project is a real treat! Help your child locate an object from home that has special meaning to him or her. Then have your child color or decorate the sign on this page, cut it out, and tape or glue it to a gift bag, grocery bag, or paper lunch bag. Help your child practice an oral description of the special object and then pack it into the bag.

We hope to see the project by _____.

Sincerely,

_____

> It's not a **trick**,
>
> But a **treat**,
>
> To share something
>
> That's really **neat!**
>
> Name _____

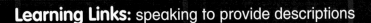

Learning Links: speaking to provide descriptions

©The Mailbox® • *Organize October Now!*™ • TEC60976

Note to the teacher: Date and sign a copy of the page. Make student copies on white construction paper; then write a child's name on a sign before sending it home with her. When a child returns her project, help her share it with the class. If desired, create a table display of all the items.

Fall

Literacy

Colorful Fall

Celebrate the many colors of the fall season with these vibrant student-made booklets! To make a booklet, cut 4" x 9" white, red, orange, yellow, and brown construction paper strips for each student. Program the white strip with the title as shown. Staple the strips together behind the title page.

Discuss with youngsters some signs of the fall season, such as leaves, pumpkins, apples, and scarecrows. Then give each student a booklet and a black crayon or marker.

For each page, have her draw a picture of a fall item that corresponds with the page's color. Help her write the color word and item name on each page. Invite youngsters to share their booklets with the class and then take them home to read to their families.

Positional words

In the Right Direction

Youngsters' positional-word skills take shape with this small-group activity! In advance, collect a class supply of fall-related objects such as acorns, pinecones, or leaves. Give each child one of the fall items. Announce a direction that includes a positional word such as "Place the acorn above your head" or "Place the leaf next to your chair." Then switch roles and give each youngster a chance to give a direction.

Graphing • **Math**

A Leafy Graph

Graphing is a breeze with this center activity! Use the patterns on page 22 to make a supply of red, brown, and yellow leaf cutouts. Store the leaves in a basket or similar container. Also make a class supply of the graph on page 22. Place the graphs, leaves, and crayons at a center.

When a child visits the center, she chooses ten leaves from the basket and sorts them by color. Then she uses corresponding crayon colors to complete the graph with her findings. If desired, invite students to share their results with a partner by using comparative words such as *most, least,* or *equal.*

Literacy • • • • • • • • • • • • • • • • • • • **Writing sentences**

Crafty Creations

Take students outside to collect different types, colors, and sizes of leaves. Back in the classroom, have each youngster choose his favorite leaf. Then have him glue the leaf to a large sheet of paper and draw a picture that incorporates the leaf in its design. Direct each student to write or dictate a sentence about his creation on a separate sentence strip. Staple the sentence to the bottom of the picture. Encourage students to share their sentences and then display their crafty creations for all to see!

Literacy

Branching Out

To prepare for this center, trim two large sheets of brown construction paper into two large-branched trees. Program a supply of leaf cutouts (patterns on page 22) with various uppercase and lowercase letters. Store the leaves in a basket or similar container. Place the basket and trees at a center. A child sorts the leaves by uppercase and lowercase letters, each on a different tree. If desired, program other sets of leaves with different sorting skills such as odd and even numbers, rhyming words, or initial sounds.

Nonstandard measurement • • • • • • • • • • • • • • • **Math**

Leafy Lengths

For each twosome, make a construction paper copy of the leaf measuring tape on page 23 and a copy of the recording sheet on page 24. Have each pair cut and glue the pieces of the measuring tape where indicated. Next, direct each duo to use the leaf tape to measure each object that is pictured on the recording sheet. Then have the pair write the results on their paper. After everyone has finished, invite youngsters to share their results. To conclude, discuss why some measurements for the same object may vary. (For example, pencils can be different sizes.)

Crisp Collections

Bring the outdoors inside with this small-group activity! In advance, ask students to bring from home some acorns, leaves, or pinecones. Place each collection in a different area of the classroom. Designate each collection with one of the following counting patterns: twos, fives, or tens. Divide students into three groups and have each group gather around a different collection. Direct youngsters to count the objects as designated. Then have the groups rotate around the room, counting the other collections by their assigned counting patterns until each group is back at its original collection. After completing the activity, make sure your little naturalists return their items to nature!

Literacy • • • • • • • • • • • • • • • *Alphabetical order*

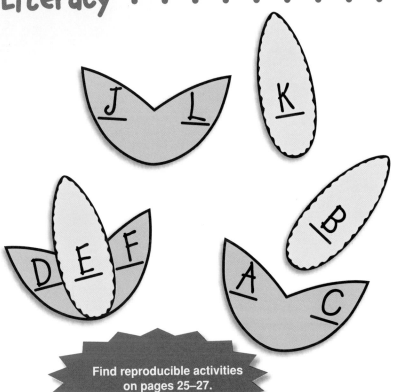

Find reproducible activities on pages 25–27.

"A-maize-ing" Matching

Here's a "corny" center packed with letter-sequencing practice! Use the corn patterns on page 24 to make the same number of yellow ears of corn and green husks. Place an ear atop a husk and program a three-letter sequence on the lines. Continue programming the cutouts with different letter sequences. Store the cutouts in a resealable plastic bag. Then place the bag at a center along with an alphabet chart.

When a youngster visits the center, he chooses a husk and finds the ear of corn with the letter that completes the sequence. Then he checks the sequence by referring to the alphabet chart. He continues in this manner for the remaining cutouts. If desired, program additional patterns with numerals for number-sequencing practice.

Leaf Patterns

Use with "A Leafy Graph" on page 19
and "Branching Out" on page 20.

©The Mailbox® • *Organize October Now!*™ • TEC60976

— Graphing

FALLEN LEAVES

Name _____

	red	brown	yellow
10			
9			
8			
7			
6			
5			
4			
3			
2			
1			

©The Mailbox® • *Organize October Now!*™ • TEC60976

Note to the teacher: Use with "A Leafy Graph" on page 19.

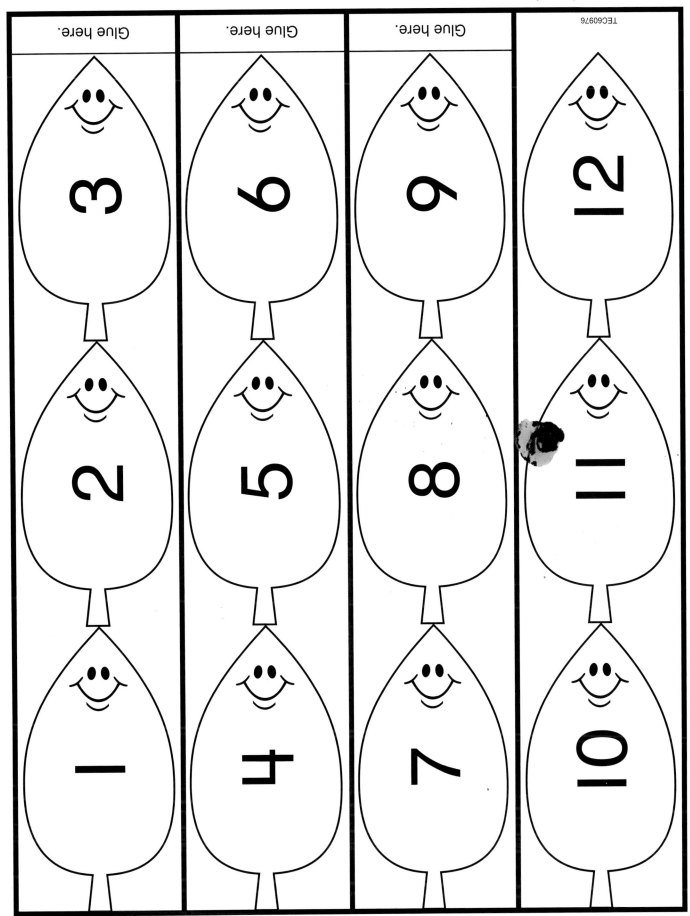

Glue here.   Glue here.   Glue here.   TEC60976

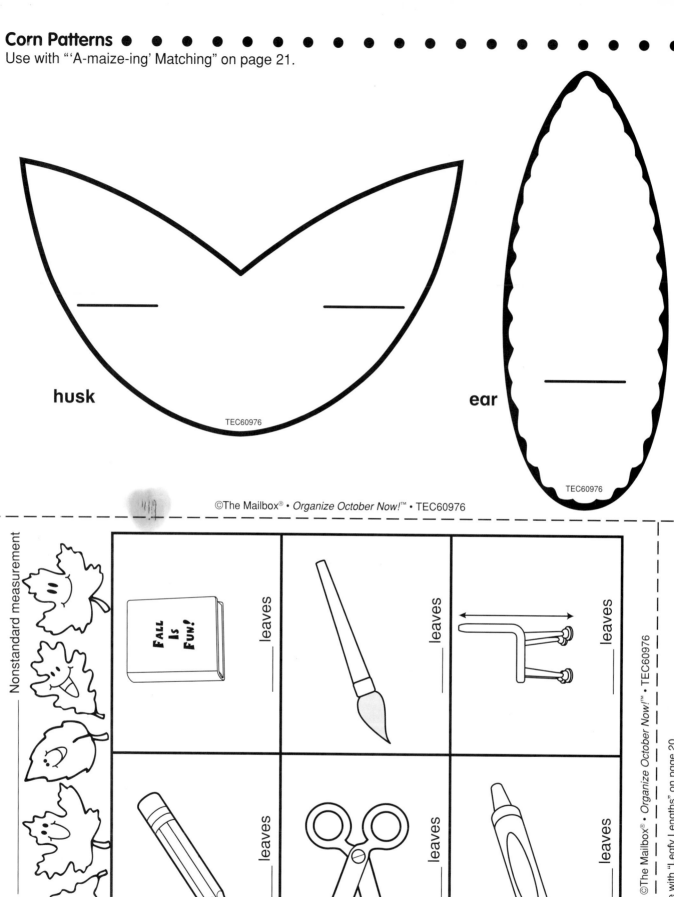

husk

ear

TEC60976

TEC60976

Nonstandard measurement

Name(s)

leaves

FALL Is FUN!

leaves

leaves

leaves

leaves

leaves

Note to the teacher: Use with "Leafy Lengths" on page 20.

24 Fall

In the Haystack

Name _____

Circle the letters in (red).

Circle the numbers in (blue).

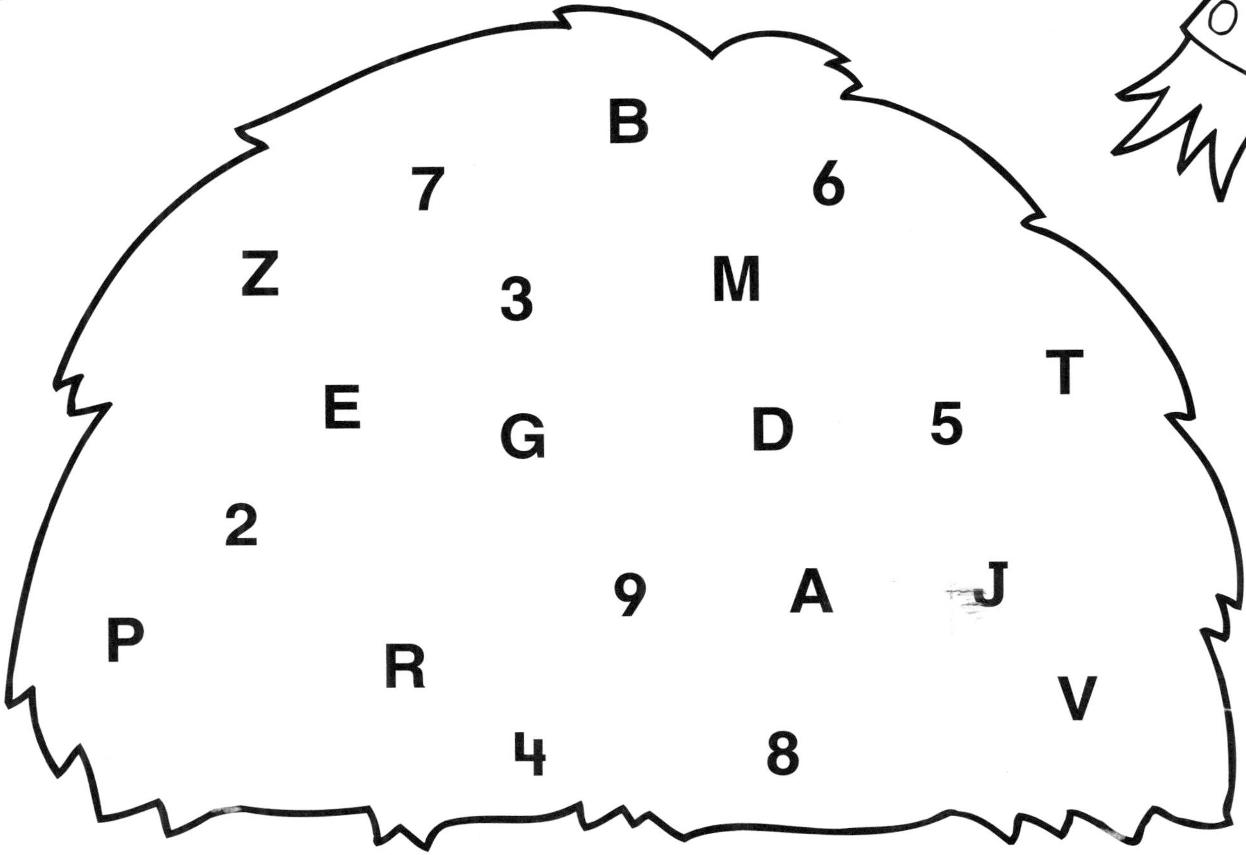

Z   E   G   7

     3   B

2   M   6

    R   D   5   T

P   4   9   A   J

       8   V

Fall Gathering

Name _____

✏️ Write the beginning letter.

🖍️ Color by the code.

Color Code
f—yellow   g—brown

_____an	_____ate	_____ox	_____eet
_____um	_____ish	_____oat	_____ork
_____ift	_____ive	_____ame	_____as

Initial Consonants: *f, g*

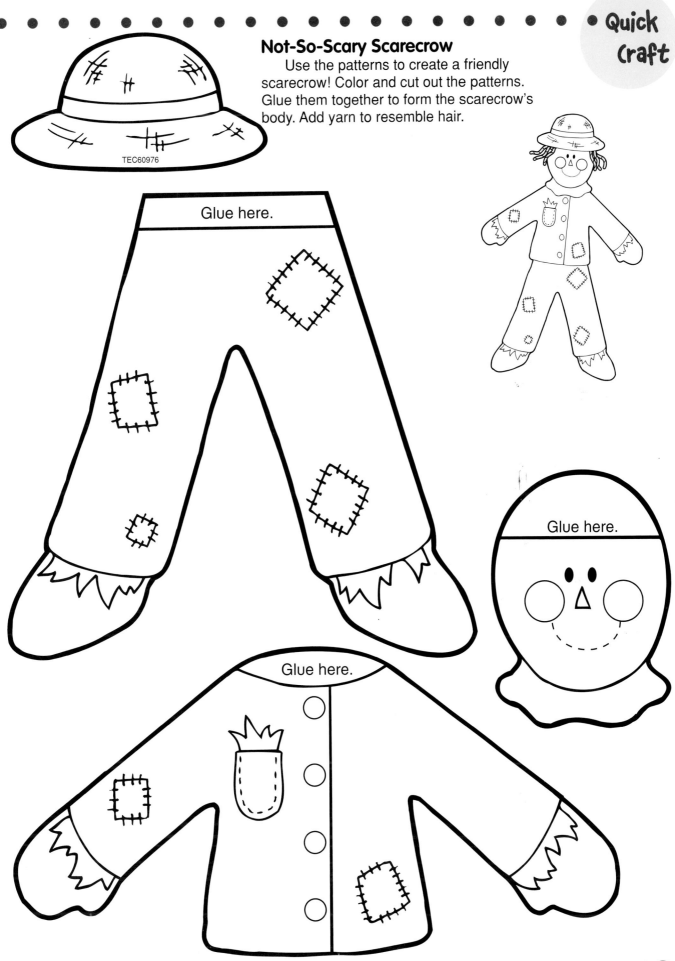

Not-So-Scary Scarecrow

Use the patterns to create a friendly scarecrow! Color and cut out the patterns. Glue them together to form the scarecrow's body. Add yarn to resemble hair.

TEC60976

Glue here.

Glue here.

Glue here.

Pumpkins

Rhyme-Time Pumpkins

Harvest bushels of rhyming practice at this partner center. Color and cut out a copy of the rhyming picture cards on page 32. Glue each card to a pumpkin cutout (pattern on page 53); then tape a craft stick to the back of each pumpkin. Store the pumpkins in a container and place the container and a block of floral foam at a center. A child chooses two pumpkins, says each picture's name, and determines whether the names rhyme. If they rhyme, he pokes the sticks into the foam block. If the names do not rhyme, he returns the pumpkins to the container and chooses two more pumpkins. He continues in this manner until all of the rhyming pairs have been planted!

Patterns • • • • • • • • • • • • • • Math

Pumpkin Patch Patterns

Cut three pumpkin shapes from thick sponges. Set out three shallow pans of different-colored paint. Use the supplies to make a few different pattern samples on paper strips. Then place the samples, the paint pans, markers, and a supply of paper strips at a center. A child chooses a sample strip, names its pattern, and then uses the stampers to re-create the pattern on her own strip. After the paint has dried, she uses a marker to draw a face on each pumpkin.

A visit to this pumpkin patch reveals a
multitude of skills just perfect for your youngsters!

Ordinal Count

This large-group game is just "ripe" for ordinal number practice! Gather students in a circle and announce an ordinal number from 1st to 10th. Hand one child a miniature pumpkin (or a pumpkin cutout) and say, "First." Direct that student to pass the pumpkin to the child on his right as the class says, "Second." Have students continue passing the pumpkin and counting by ordinal numbers until they reach the stated number. Then have the child in the featured position move to the middle of the circle for one round. Announce a new ordinal number and repeat the activity.

Literacy • • • • • • • • • • • • • • • • • *True or false*

Pumpkin Facts

To prepare, write on strips of paper the pumpkin statements shown and place them in a container. Also give each child an orange construction paper pumpkin cutout (pattern on page 53) and have him decorate it as desired. Then help him tape a craft stick to the back for a handle. To play, draw a strip from the container and read the statement. If the statement is true, students hold up their pumpkins. If the statement is false, they keep their pumpkins in their laps. Continue in this manner until all of the statements have been read.

True pumpkin statements:
Pumpkins have seeds.
Pumpkins are orange.
Pumpkins grow on vines.
Pumpkins have stems.

False pumpkin statements:
Pumpkins can grow legs.
Pumpkins can talk.
Pumpkins are purple.
There is only one seed inside a pumpkin.

Literacy

Jack-o'-Lantern in the Window

Give each child four 3" x 5" yellow construction paper cards and a 9" x 12" sheet of black construction paper. Have each child draw a jack-o'-lantern on one of the cards. On each of the other three cards, have him write a sentence to describe his jack-o'-lantern's shape, color, or facial expression. Then instruct him to glue the cards to the black paper, as shown, to resemble a window. Invite each child to share his work with the group before posting the projects for all to see.

Comparing sets • • • • • • • • • • • • • • • • # Math

Pumpkins in the Patch

Youngsters compare the number of pumpkins in the patch at this partner center. To prepare, draw vines and leaves on two sheets of paper to create gameboards. Place the boards, a supply of orange pom-poms (pumpkins), and a pair of large dice at a center. To play, each child rolls a die and places the corresponding number of pumpkins on her gameboard. The duo compares the two numbers and determines who has more, who has less, or whether the sets are equal. Then each child clears her board and the twosome repeats the activity. Play continues as time allows.

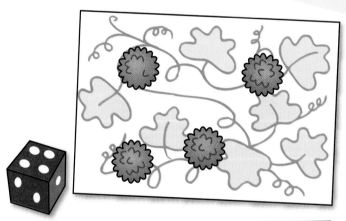

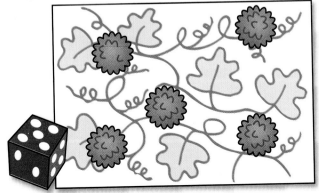

Pumpkin Tallies

Display a pumpkin and tell students that they will vote to determine what type of face to give it. Have students brainstorm a list of expressions or feelings. Draw and label each expression on the board. Next, have each child cast her vote by drawing her chosen expression on an orange pumpkin cutout and then depositing it in a container. After all the votes are cast, remove each ballot and use tally marks to record the votes on the board. Enlist students' help in determining the totals and comparing the numbers to identify the winning choice. Then decorate or carve the pumpkin to resemble the type of face illustrated by the majority of children.

Jack-o'-Lantern Slide

This partner center brightens students' vocabularies! Use the patterns on page 33 to make an even number of orange jack-o'-lantern shapes and a matching number of yellow tachistoscope strips. Program each strip with sight words. Laminate the strips and patterns for durability. Cut out the shapes. Use a craft knife to slit the dashed lines on each jack-o'-lantern and then insert a strip as shown. Place the projects at a center. Each partner, in turn, takes a jack-o'-lantern and reads the sight words while his partner verifies his reading. They continue with each remaining jack-o'-lantern.

Find reproducible activities on pages 34–35.

TEC60976

A Full Load

Name _____

Color Code

△—yellow   ○—red

□—blue   □—green

 Color.
Use the code.

✏ Write how many.

Shapes

Order in the Patch

Name _____

1 2 3 4 5 6 7 8 9 10

✏️ Write the numbers in order.

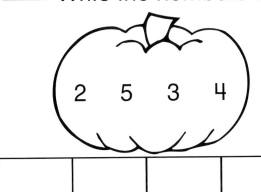

2 5 3 4

9 7 8 6

10 8 7 9

4 6 5 7

3 1 4 2

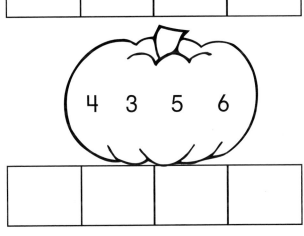

4 3 5 6

Spiders

Literacy

Miss Muffet's Meal

No doubt Miss Muffet would abandon her curds and whey if she were to see this class book, which recommends tastier meal options! Recite the traditional nursery rhyme "Little Miss Muffet," encouraging students to join in. Explain that curds and whey is a food that is similar to cottage cheese. Then have students suggest other foods that Miss Muffet might enjoy more than curds and whey. Next, give each child a sheet of paper programmed with the prompt shown, excluding the information in the blank. Have him choose a favorite food and write its name in the blank. Then encourage him to draw a picture above the text. Staple the completed pages together with a cover titled "Meals for Miss Muffet."

Meals for Miss Muffet

Little Miss Muffet sat on a tuffet Eating her _macaroni and cheese_.

Story problems

Math

Spiffy Spider Socks

This spider is having a difficult time deciding how many socks it needs for its chilly feet! Enlist youngsters' help in solving the spider's dilemma with fancy footwear manipulation. Give each child a copy of page 40. Have her color the spider and socks and then cut out the cards. Read the story problem shown. Have each child place each of four socks on a different foot. Encourage her to count the number of feet that still need socks. Then have her share the answer. Repeat the activity several times, substituting a different number in the second line each time.

This spider's feet are cold! It has [four] socks on. How many more socks does it need?

Literacy

Beginning sound /s/

Leggy Learning

Make a copy of the spider body and picture cards on page 41. Color and cut out the patterns. Tape each card to an end of a different black tagboard strip (leg). A child chooses a leg and decides whether the picture's name begins with /s/. If it does, he positions the leg on the spider. If the picture's name does not begin with /s/, he puts the leg aside. After he has reviewed all of the legs, he checks his work by counting to see whether the spider has eight legs.

Math

Sorting by size

Web, Sweet Web

Use a black marker to draw a web on each of three paper plates to make sorting mats. Copy the spider cards on page 42; then cut them out and store them in a resealable plastic bag. Place the bag and the sorting mats at a center. A child sorts the spiders by size onto the webs. To create a more challenging center, randomly color the cards so that three different colors are represented. Then children can sort the spiders two different ways: by size and by color.

Piggyback Babies

Youngsters may be surprised to find out that some spiders carry their young on their backs! Put this fascinating fact to good use with this center! To make mother spiders, enlarge the spider card on page 40 and make two copies. Cut out the cards, color them, and label them as shown. Make a supply of the medium spider cards from page 42 to represent spiderlings. Label each card with a different numeral. Then place the prepared items at a center. After sharing the fact above with your youngsters, encourage children to visit the center in pairs. Have the visiting students take turns identifying the numeral on each spiderling and placing it on the back of a mother spider to identify the numeral as odd or even.

Spider Search

Send your youngsters on a search for colorful spiders. Use a reduced copy of the spider card on page 40 to make a recording sheet, similar to the one shown, that depicts five stationary objects in your classroom. Also use the card to make five construction paper spiders in different colors. Tape each spider to a different object shown on the recording sheet. Give each child a recording sheet and have him search the room for spiders. When he locates a spider, instruct him to find the corresponding sentence on his sheet and write the appropriate color word in the blank. After he has located all the spiders, have him read each sentence.

Spider Specifics

Have each child glue construction paper circles in an overlapping formation, as shown, to make a spider body. Encourage him to glue eight accordion-folded strips to the body to resemble legs. Then have him add two sticky-dot eyes and a construction paper mouth to complete the spider. Have each child think of a name for his spider and write it on an index card along with a sentence or two about the arachnid. Instruct him to glue the card to the center of his spider. To showcase students' work, attach fake spiderwebs to a bulletin board and add the spiders.

Spooky
My spidr is purpl.
He liks to eat lots of flys.
Andy

Math • • • • • • • • • • • • • • • • • *Identifying numerals*

Fabulous Flies

Use a marker to program each of ten paper plates with a different number from 1 to 10. Draw a web around the number on each plate. Also draw a small spider on each web. Place the plates and a supply of small black pom-poms (flies) at a center. A child selects a web and names its number. Then she counts and places the corresponding number of flies on the web. She continues in the same way for each remaining web.

Find a reproducible activity on page 43.

Use with "Spiffy Spider Socks" on page 36 and "Piggyback Babies" and "Spider Search" on page 38.

TEC60976

Sock Cards

Use with "Spiffy Spider Socks" on page 36.

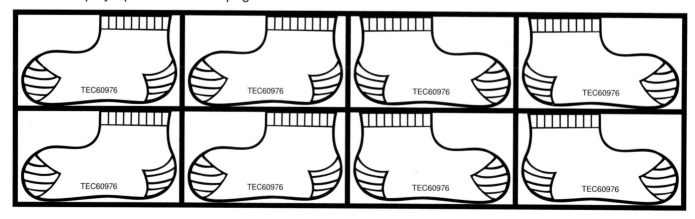

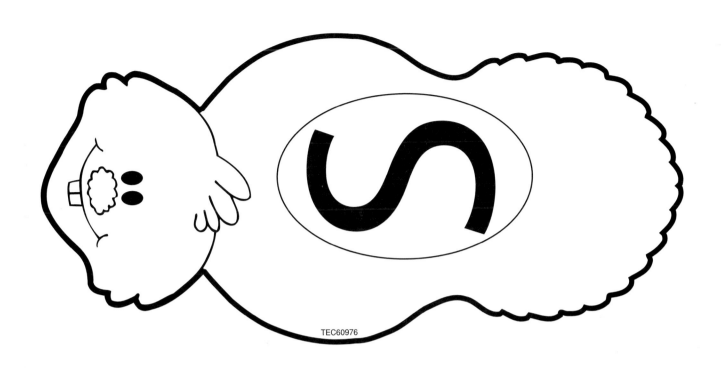

TEC60976

Spider Cards

Use with "Web, Sweet Web" on page 37 and "Piggyback Babies" on page 38.

TEC60976

TEC60976

TEC60976

TEC60976

TEC60976

TEC60976

TEC60976

TEC60976

TEC60976

TEC60976

TEC60976

TEC60976

TEC60976

TEC60976

TEC60976

A Wonderful Web

Name _____

 Cut.

Glue the pictures whose names begin with **w**.

 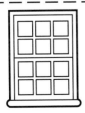    

Fire Safety

Rules to Remember

Discuss with youngsters ways to prevent fires and how to stay safe in case of a fire. Then give each student a copy of page 47 and have him color and cut out the fire station and booklet pages. Direct him to sequence the pages and staple them atop the fire station as shown. Encourage youngsters to read the text along with you, tracking each word as it's read. Have students explain what Blaze does wrong on pages 1–3 and what he does right on page 4. Invite youngsters to read their booklets with partners before they take them home to share with their families.

FIRE STATION
5
Play It Safe, Blaze

by Ethan

Fiery Facts

Your junior firefighters save the day during this group activity! Trim bulletin board paper into a house shape and mount it within students' reach. Cut out a supply of construction paper flames similar to the ones shown. Lightly tape the flames to the house.

Gather students around the display and announce a true or false statement about fire safety (see suggestions shown). Have students decide whether the statement is true or false. If the statement is true, invite a volunteer to remove a flame from the house. Continue in this manner until all of the flames have been extinguished.

True
You should test your smoke alarms.
Fire is hot.
Call 9-1-1 for an emergency.
Plan an escape route from your house.
Fires can be dangerous.
Smoke from a fire can make you sick.

False
It is safe to play with matches.
Your home does not need smoke alarms.
Fires are cold.
It is safe for children to use the stove.
Fires cannot hurt you.

These red-hot activities are just what you need to set your classroom ablaze with learning!

Addition • Math

To the Rescue!

Ignite students' interest in comparing numbers with this two-player addition game! Give each youngster a copy of the house pattern and game marker on page 48 to color and cut out. Have her fold the game marker on the lines and tape the bottom flaps together to make a standing game piece. Each twosome also needs two dice, a sheet of scrap paper, and a pencil.

To play, each player places her firefighter game marker at the bottom of her ladder. The first player rolls the dice and adds the numbers together on the scrap paper. The other player takes a turn in the same manner. Then the youngsters compare their sums. The player with the larger sum moves her firefighter up one ladder rung. Play continues until a player reaches the top of the ladder.

Literacy • • • • • • • • • • • • • • Convey a message through pictures

Staying Safe

This eye-catching door display showers students with safety reminders! Cut a large hydrant, hose, and nozzle from bulletin board paper. Mount the cutouts as shown. Attach blue crepe paper strips to the end of the nozzle to resemble streams of water. Also prepare a class supply of water droplet cutouts.

Ask students to name dangerous items that can cause fires, such as an iron, a stove, a fireplace, a match, and a candle. Then have each child draw a picture of a dangerous item on a droplet. Display the droplets on the door as fire safety reminders.

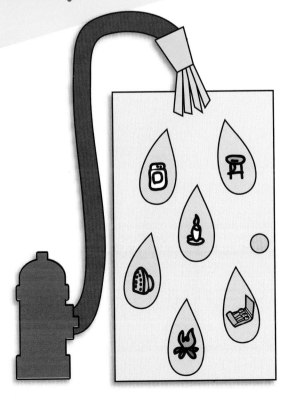

Fire Safety 45

Literacy · · · · · · · · · · · · · · · · · · ·

Delightful Dalmatians

These cute canines help youngsters remember that *dalmatian* begins with *d*! Have each child cut two ears from white construction paper and glue one to each side of a nine-inch white paper plate. After drawing facial features to resemble a dalmatian, have each youngster dip a large pom-pom into black paint and repeatedly press it on the plate to make spots. When the paint is dry, tape a large craft stick handle to the back of the dalmatian.

To begin, review the sound of *d.* Then say a word aloud. If the word begins with /d/, a student holds up her dalmatian. If it does not, she sits quietly with her puppet in her lap. Continue in this manner with additional words.

One-to-one correspondence · · · · · · · · · · · · · · · Math

Firefighting

For this partner game, copy the counters below to make six flames and six pails for each student pair. Assign one child in each twosome to be Fire and the other child to be Water. Have each partner color and cut out her game counters and place them in a stack.

To play, Fire rolls a large die and lays out the corresponding number of flame counters. Next, Water rolls the die, counts out the corresponding number of water pails, and attempts to place a pail on each flame. Then the twosome describes the outcome using words such as *more, less,* and *same.* Play continues in this manner with the partners switching roles after each round.

Find a reproducible activity on page 49.

Game Counters
Use with "Firefighting" on this page.

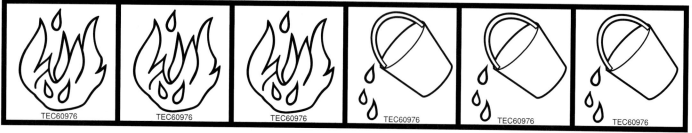

TEC60976	TEC60976	TEC60976	TEC60976	TEC60976	TEC60976

©The Mailbox® · *Organize October Now!*™ · TEC60976

FIRE STATION
5

Yes, Blaze! Good dog. 4

Play It Safe,
Blaze

by _____

©The Mailbox® • *Organize October Now!*™ • TEC60976

No, Blaze! No! 1

No, Blaze! No! 2

No, Blaze! No! 3

TEC60976

TEC60976

The Hose Knows

Name _____

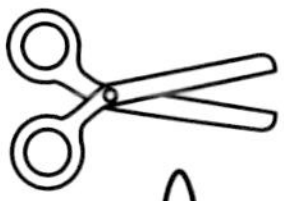

✂ Cut.

🍶 Glue from shortest to longest to make a hose.

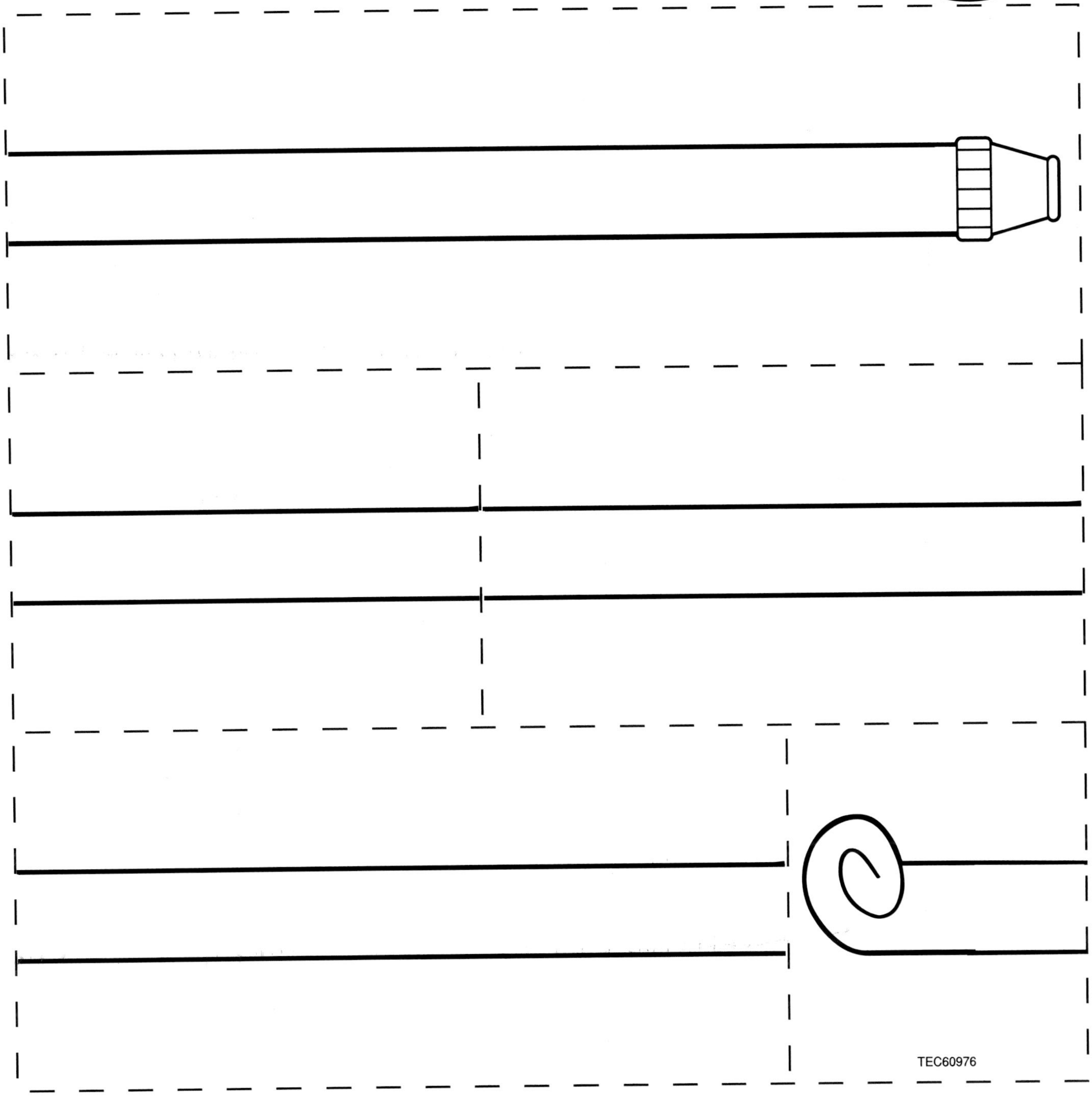

TEC60976

Note to the teacher: Have each child glue the hoses on a 3" x 24" strip of paper.

Order by Length **49**

Arts & Crafts

Autumn Splendor

Bring the beauty of fall into your classroom with this vivid project! To make one, color a copy of the tree pattern on page 52. Press a finger in a shallow pan of red tempera paint and make multiple fingerprints on the tree branches to resemble leaves. Repeat the process with additional fall colors of paint. Allow the paint to dry and then add crayon details.

Shapely Fire Trucks

To make a fire truck, position red, yellow, and black construction paper shapes on a sheet of white construction paper to resemble a fire truck as shown; then glue the shapes in place. Add details to the truck and the surrounding scene with crayons, markers, or paper scraps.

Jack-o'-Lantern Faces

To make this unique table topper, cut out a construction paper copy of the pumpkins on page 53 and embellish each one with facial features. Glue all four of the pumpkins back-to-back as shown. Punch a hole in the tops of the pumpkins. Then tie several lengths of curling ribbon through the holes to resemble vines. Next, glue fall leaves to a small paper plate. (Plastic or silk leaves may be used if desired.) Glue the pumpkins on top of the leaves. Allow time for the glue to dry. Then decorate tables in your classroom with the toppers.

Gluey Ghost

There's nothing scary about these cute suncatcher ghosts! To make one, pour a small amount of white glue on a piece of waxed paper. Pick up the paper and tilt it slightly until the glue moves into a desired shape. After the glue is dry, carefully peel it from the waxed paper. Use a permanent marker to draw eyes and a mouth. Then attach the resulting ghosts to a sunny window.

TEC60976

©The Mailbox® • *Organize October Now!*™ • TEC60976

52 Arts & Crafts

Note to the teacher: Use with "Autumn Splendor" on page 50.

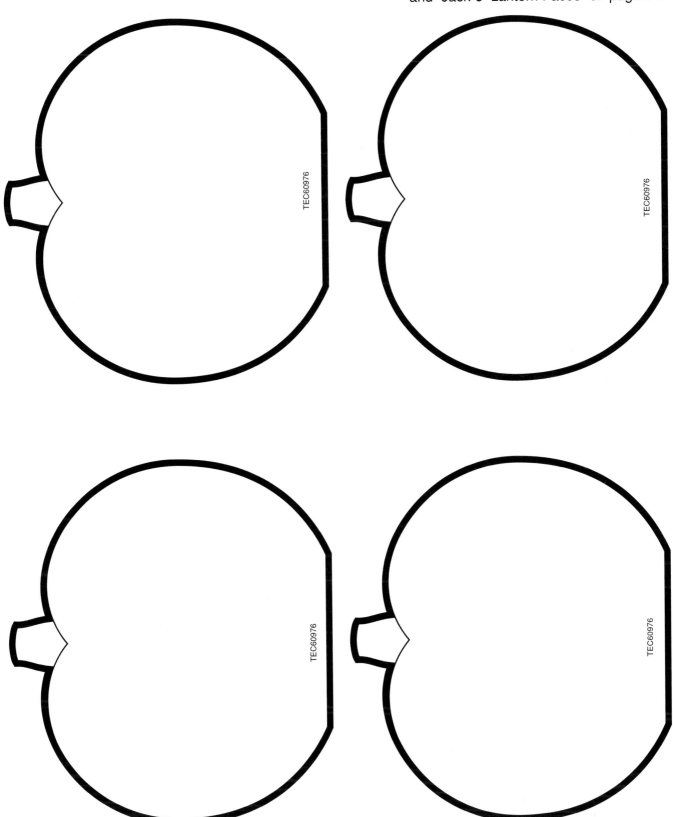

TEC60976

TEC60976

TEC60976

TEC60976

Cultivate youngsters' joy of reading with pleasing pumpkins! Title a bulletin board as shown. Use a marker to draw vines under the title. Have children cut out green construction paper leaves. Then staple the leaves to the vines. Place a supply of orange construction paper pumpkin cutouts and a black marker near the board. Each time a student reads a book, have him write the book's title and his name on a cutout. Staple each completed pumpkin to the patch.

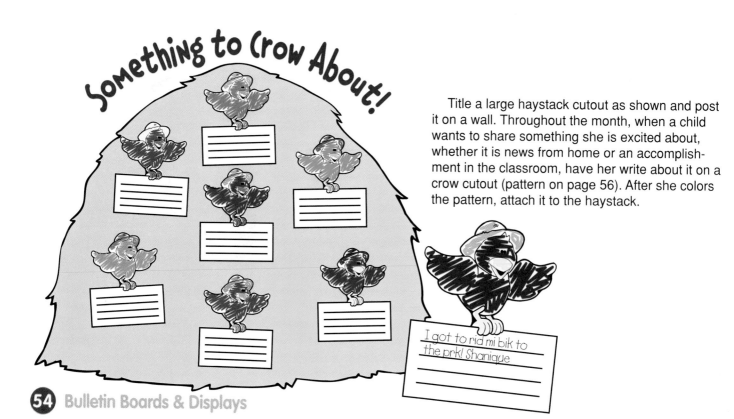

Title a large haystack cutout as shown and post it on a wall. Throughout the month, when a child wants to share something she is excited about, whether it is news from home or an accomplishment in the classroom, have her write about it on a crow cutout (pattern on page 56). After she colors the pattern, attach it to the haystack.

Displays

After reviewing information on fire safety, give each youngster a red construction paper copy of the hat pattern on page 57. Instruct each child to write a rule for fire safety on his hat. Invite each child to share his writing; then display the hats on a bulletin board. If desired, embellish the board with a fire hose and hydrant cutout and the title shown.

Student work is on display with this Halloween bulletin board! Paint the bottom of each child's foot with white paint; then press her foot on black construction paper to make a print. After the paint is dry, have her use a marker to sign her name and draw a face on her print to resemble a ghost. Cut out the completed ghosts and staple them along with student work to the board.

Crow Pattern

Use with "Something to Crow About!" on page 54.

TEC60976

Fire
Dept.

Centers

Shapes

Geometric Jacks

Cut out a large pumpkin from orange construction paper and a large supply of simple black construction paper shapes to use as facial features. Store the shapes in a small trick-or-treat bag. Make several cards, similar to the ones shown, with guidelines for creating jack-o'-lanterns. Place the cards at a center along with the pumpkin mat and the bag. A child chooses a card and uses the guidelines to create a jack-o'-lantern. After a classmate verifies his work, he clears his mat and repeats the activity with another card.

Use

1 ■

2 ●s

5 ▲s

to make a face!

Use

1 ●

2 ▲s

5 ■s

to make a face!

Uppercase and lowercase letters

Literacy

Just Add Wings

For this letter-matching center, make several construction paper copies of the bat patterns on page 60. For each bat, write the corresponding uppercase and lowercase letters on the wings. Laminate and cut out the pieces; then use a permanent marker to program the backs of the cutouts for self-checking. Store the cutouts in a large envelope decorated like a bat cave. A child matches each uppercase and lowercase letter and then flips the cutouts to check her work.

Addition

Take Aim!

Cut out a jumbo-size leaf, divide it into five sections, and label each section with a different number from 1 to 5. Place the cutout and two large pom-poms on the floor in an open area. A child tosses the pom-poms onto the leaf. Then, on a sheet of paper, he writes the numbers (in the form of an addition sentence) where the pom-poms landed. He solves the fact and repeats the activity until he's written and answered a designated number of facts.

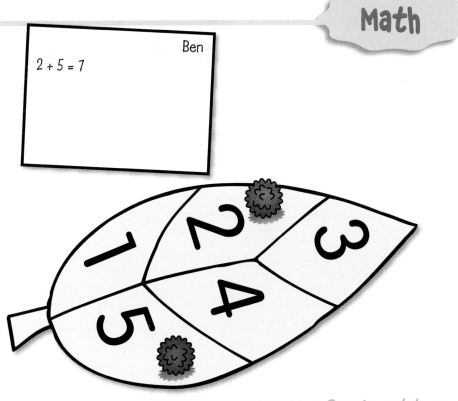

Ben

$2 + 5 = 7$

Literacy

Onsets and rimes

Word-Family Pumpkins

Make several orange construction paper copies of the pattern and letter cards on page 61. Write a different rime on each pumpkin as shown. (Consider rimes such as -at, -et, -op, and -ad.) Cut out the pumpkins and cards on each page and store each set in a separate resealable plastic bag. A child chooses a bag and places each letter card, in turn, in the space provided and reads aloud the resulting word. If it is a real word, she leaves the card on the pumpkin. If it is not a real word, she sets the card aside. She continues in this manner for each bag.

Bat Patterns

Use with "Just Add Wings" on page 58.

TEC60976

TEC60976

TEC60976

c	m	p	b
t	d	f	s

Counting to ten

One, two, three, four, five, six...

Halloween Corners!

Youngsters release their wiggles when playing this indoor recess game. To begin, label each corner of your classroom with a different seasonal name, such as "Bat Cave," "Scarecrow's Field," "Pumpkin Patch," and "Haunted House." Choose a student to be It; then have this student close her eyes and count to ten out loud. During this time, each of the remaining students quietly moves to the corner of her choice. After calling the number ten, It calls a corner's name and opens her eyes. All the students in the called corner must return to their desks. Play continues in this manner until only one player remains standing. This player becomes the new It and all seated students rejoin the game.

Visual discrimination

Literacy

Make a Monster

There will be giggles galore as youngsters eagerly create these unique monsters. Cut out a copy of the monster facial feature cards on page 64. Shuffle the cards and place them in a basket. Divide youngsters into two teams. For each team, draw an oval (a head) on the chalkboard. To play, choose a youngster from each team to be the artist. Have each artist choose a card and then draw the indicated part on his team's monster. When both artists are finished, continue play by choosing a new artist from each team. If an artist chooses a body part that has already been completed on his team's monster, he puts the card back in the basket and returns to his team. Play continues until each of the monsters is complete.

Spelling Football

Score big with this large-group spelling game! To create a playing field, draw a line down the center of the chalkboard and label it "50." On each side of the line, draw and label lines that represent ten-yard increments from 40 to 0. Display two football cutouts (pattern on page 65) on the 50-yard line and divide the class into two teams. Alternating between the teams, call upon individual players to spell a word. (For younger students, have them spell their names.) If the player correctly spells the word, his team's football advances ten yards. When a touchdown is scored, both teams celebrate, and the scoring team's football is returned to the 50 yard line. The game continues until every player participates one or more times.

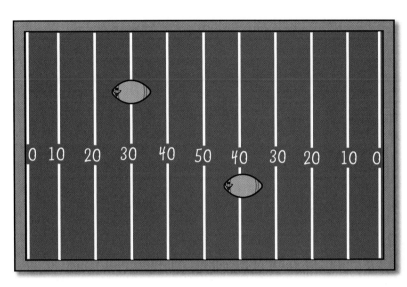

Boo!

Scare up plenty of basic-fact practice playing this small-group game! Make seven copies of the ghost cards on page 65. Program three cards with "Boo!" Program the remaining cards with an unanswered math fact appropriate for your students. Cut out the cards and place them in a plastic pumpkin or trick-or-treat bag. To play, one student in the group draws a card, reads the fact aloud, and provides its answer. If the group agrees that the answer is correct, he keeps the card. If his answer is incorrect, he returns the card. Then he passes the container to the classmate on his left. Play continues in this manner. When a player draws a Boo! card, he must return all his cards to the container, including the Boo! card. The student who has the most cards at the end of the game time wins.

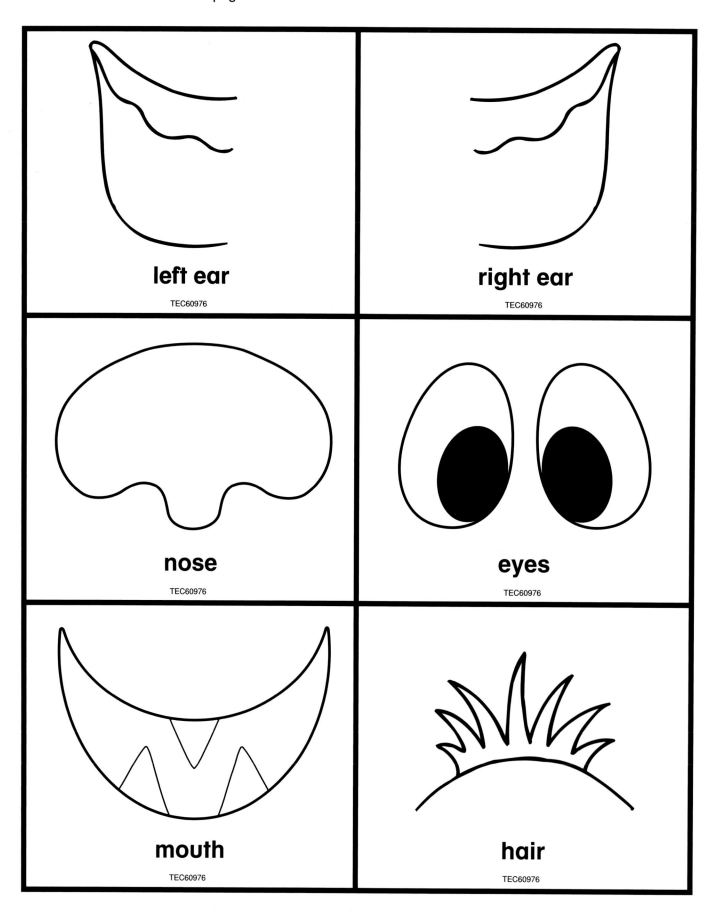

left ear

TEC60976

right ear

TEC60976

nose

TEC60976

eyes

TEC60976

mouth

TEC60976

hair

TEC60976

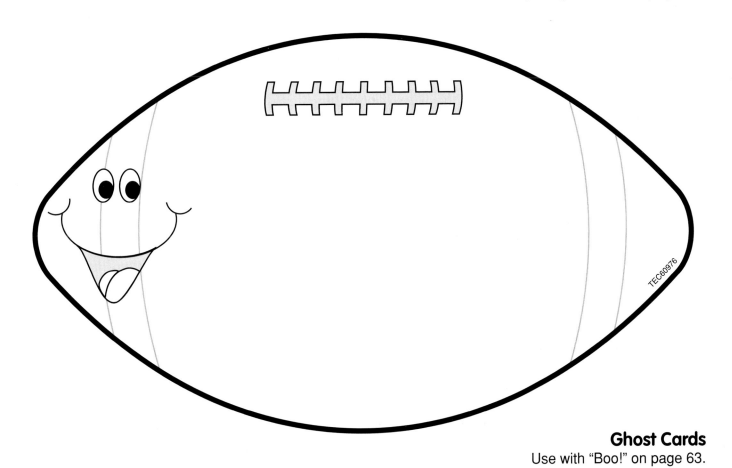

TEC60976

Ghost Cards
Use with "Boo!" on page 63.

TEC60976   TEC60976   TEC60976   TEC60976

Management Tips

Good Behavior Motivator

Reinforce positive behavior with an idea that's the pick of the patch! Draw a large pumpkin outline on a bulletin board. Then cut a stem and jack-o'-lantern features, such as eyes, a nose, and a mouth, from construction paper and store them in a container near the board. Each day that the class meets a daily behavior goal, such as walking quietly in the hall or not interrupting, invite a student to add a cutout to the display. When the jack-o'-lantern is complete, celebrate students' success with extra free time, a special snack, or another class treat!

Mr. Monster Says...

Mr. Monster's Message

Help youngsters keep important reminders top of mind with the help of a cuddly monster. Enlarge the monster pattern on page 67, color it, and post it in a prominent location. Add a laminated speech bubble and the title "Mr. Monster Says…." Each morning, use a wipe-off marker to program the speech bubble with a message. Then, during your morning group time, invite a youngster to help you read the message.

Don't forget about our field trip to the pumpkin patch tomorrow! Bring your lunch.

TEC60976

Time Fillers

Free-Time Doodles

Be prepared when students complete their work early. Cut a large fall shape, such as a pumpkin or a leaf, from bulletin board paper. Attach the cutout to a wall within students' reach. When youngsters finish their work early, encourage them to draw or write on the paper. Whenever the cutout is full, place it in the hallway for others to see.

What's Your Prediction?

When faced with a few extra minutes, draw one part of a seasonal object such as a spider, a jack-o'-lantern, or a scarecrow. Then invite two students to predict what object you are drawing. If neither prediction is correct, draw another part of the object; then stop for two more predictions. Continue in this manner until a correct prediction is made. Hey, that's a spider!

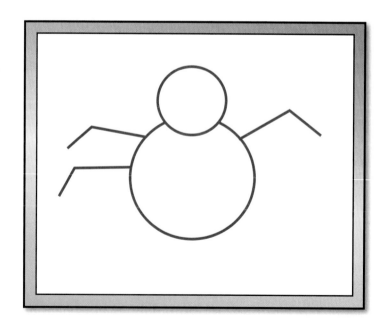

Making a List

Reserve a portion of your chalkboard for this listing activity. On individual slips of paper, write several topics for making lists, such as "Treats Received When Trick-or-Treating," "Items That Are Orange," and "Words Associated With Halloween." Place the slips in a decorated container on your desk. When you have a few minutes to fill, choose a topic from the container and copy it on the reserved portion of your chalkboard. Then have students name items as you list their answers on the board.

Items That Are Orange
basketball
pumpkin
orange
crayon
jack-o'-lantern
fire

"...and then I put on *my* mask. My sister started laughing instead of screaming. She didn't think I was very scary!"

The Never-Ending Tale

Whenever you have a bit of extra time, you can use it to improve your youngsters' language and storytelling skills. Begin telling a Halloween story. After a few sentences, select a child to continue the story. Encourage him to add to the story; then select another child to pick up where this storyteller leaves off. Continue the story as long as time permits, giving each child a turn.

Journal Prompts

- If you were a pumpkin in a pumpkin patch, what would you say to someone to get him or her to choose you over another pumpkin?

- Firefighters do an important job. I would like to tell all firefighters…

- If you were a scarecrow, what would you do to make the crows afraid of you?

- When trick-or-treating, always remember…

- The best thing about a cool October day is…

- If you could fly like a bat, where would you go? Why?

Use one or more of the following ideas and the bat pattern on page 72 to get students batty about writing.

- After a study of bats, have each youngster write facts about these fascinating animals on a copy of the bat pattern. Have her cut out the bat, fold its wings forward, and color it. Then display the bats on a bulletin board.

- Use the bat pattern for journal writing. Write the last journal prompt from above on a copy of the bat pattern. Add writing lines to the pattern if desired and then make a class supply.

- Have each child write a story about a pet bat on a copy of the bat pattern.

Some bats eat bugs.
Bats can hang upside down.
Bailey

Prompts

Pumpkin Possibilities

Jack-o'-lanterns and pies—what else can pumpkins be used for? No doubt youngsters will be eager to tell you with this creative-writing idea! Remind students that in the story *Cinderella,* a pumpkin is transformed into a lovely coach. Have youngsters brainstorm a list of other creative pumpkin uses. Next, give each child a 12" x 18" sheet of construction paper and a pumpkin cutout. Have him decide on an unusual use for his pumpkin. Instruct him to glue his pumpkin to the upper half of the paper and add any desired illustrations. After his picture is complete, have him describe his inventive idea in writing under his picture.

My dog likes to run away. I could tie him to a pumpkin. They could be friends.

Tommy

Courtney

My owl flies by and sees my swing set in the backyard.

Owl Eyes

"Whoooo" likes to write descriptively? Your students do with this nifty project. Make enough copies of the owl eyes on page 73 so that each child will have one set. Have each student color a set of the eyes and glue them to a brown construction paper rectangle as shown. Encourage each student to embellish her owl with craft items and then mount it on a sheet of construction paper. Instruct each child to write a caption for her picture that explains what the owl might see as it flies. Then invite each student to share her project with the class.

Bat Pattern
Use with the ideas at the bottom of page 70.

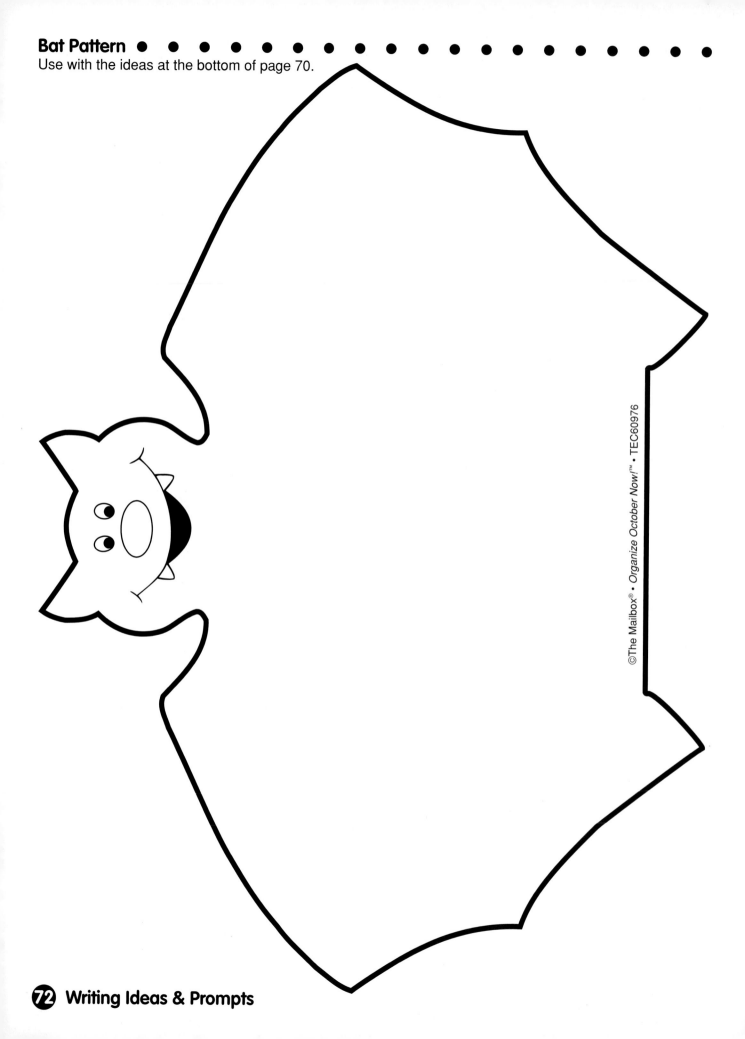

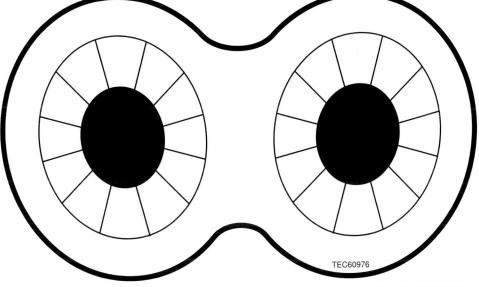

TEC60976

A Pumpkin Parade

A ready-to-use center mat and cards for two different learning levels

Materials:

center mat to the right
center cards on page 77
center cards on page 79
resealable plastic bag

Preparing the center:

Cut out the cards. To have youngsters order the numbers 1–10, place only the first set of cards in the bag. If students are working at a more advanced level, place both sets of cards in the bag to have them sequence the numbers 1–20.

Using the center:

1. A child removes the cards from the bag and lays them faceup in the center area.
2. She places the cards on the mat in order. (If she is completing the center with cards 1–20, she places cards 1–10 on the mat and then places cards 11–20 below the mat.)

Follow-Up

After a student completes the center activity for sequencing numbers to 10, use the skill sheet on page 81 for more practice.

A Pumpkin Parade

Put the cards in order.

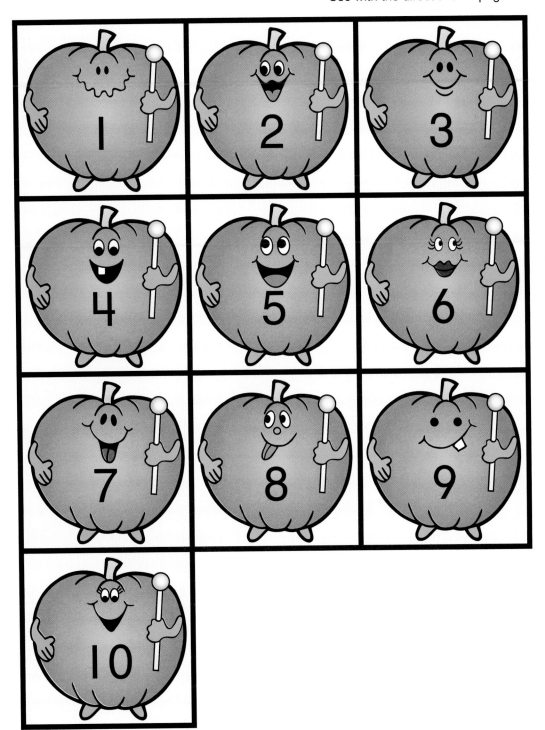

A Pumpkin Parade

TEC60976

A Pumpkin Parade

TEC60976

A Pumpkin Parade

TEC60976

A Pumpkin Parade

TEC60976

A Pumpkin Parade

TEC60976

A Pumpkin Parade

TEC60976

A Pumpkin Parade

TEC60976

A Pumpkin Parade

TEC60976

A Pumpkin Parade

TEC60976

A Pumpkin Parade

TEC60976

A Pumpkin Parade
TEC60976

A Pumpkin Parade
TEC60976

A Pumpkin Parade
TEC60976

A Pumpkin Parade
TEC60976

A Pumpkin Parade
TEC60976

A Pumpkin Parade
TEC60976

A Pumpkin Parade
TEC60976

A Pumpkin Parade
TEC60976

A Pumpkin Parade
TEC60976

A Pumpkin Parade
TEC60976

New to the Patch!

Name _____

✂ Cut.   🧴 Glue in order.

1   9

9   10   3   7

2   4
5   8

Chew a Shoe

A ready-to-use center mat and cards for two different learning levels

Materials:

center mat to the right
color cards on page 85
color cards on page 87
two resealable plastic bags

Preparing the center:

Cut out the cards and place each set in a separate bag.

Using the center:

1. A child removes the cards from one bag and lays them faceup in the center area.
2. He chooses a card, identifies the color word, and places it on top of the shoe with the corresponding color. Then he repeats the process with each remaining card.
3. To check his work, he flips over all of the cards. If the color on the back of each card matches the color of the corresponding shoe, he is finished. If not, he turns the cards over and rearranges them until they are placed correctly.

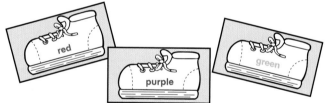

Follow-Up

After a student completes a center activity, use the skill sheet on page 89 for more practice.

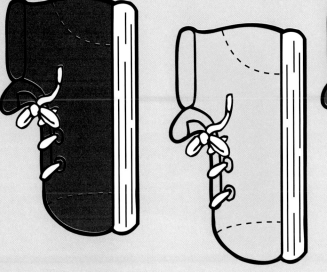

Chew a Shoe

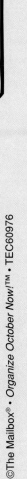

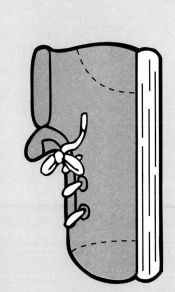

Choose a card.

Match.

Check.

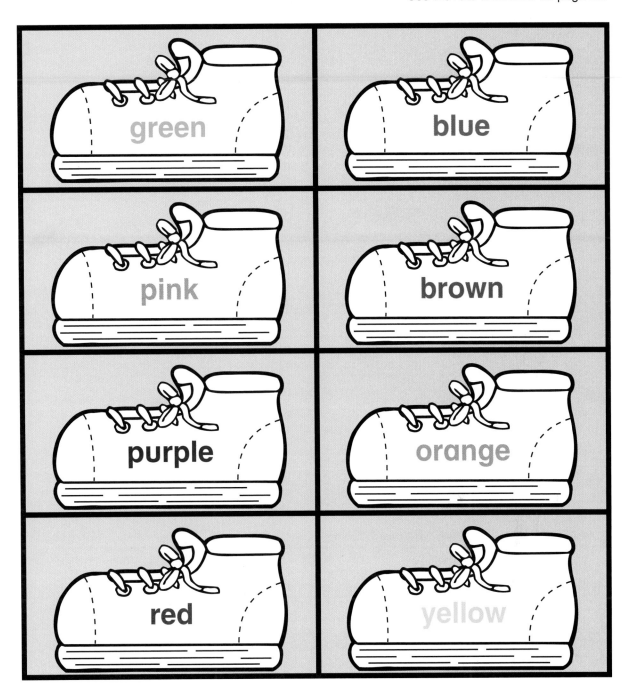

green

blue

pink

brown

purple

orange

red

yellow

Chew a Shoe **85**

Chew a Shoe
TEC60976

Chew a Shoe
TEC60976

Chew a Shoe
TEC60976

Chew a Shoe
TEC60976

Chew a Shoe
TEC60976

Chew a Shoe
TEC60976

Chew a Shoe
TEC60976

Chew a Shoe
TEC60976

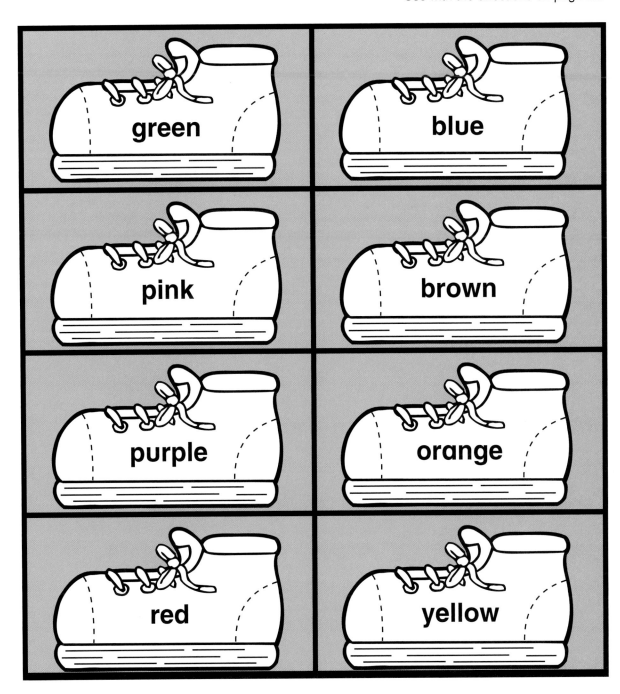

green

blue

pink

brown

purple

orange

red

yellow

Chew a Shoe **87**

Chew a Shoe
TEC60976

Chew a Shoe
TEC60976

Chew a Shoe
TEC60976

Chew a Shoe
TEC60976

Chew a Shoe
TEC60976

Chew a Shoe
TEC60976

Chew a Shoe
TEC60976

Chew a Shoe
TEC60976

Fido's Footwear

✏️ Draw lines to match each pair.

🖍️ Color.

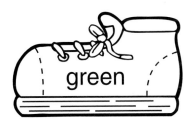 green

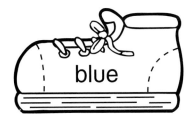 blue

 orange

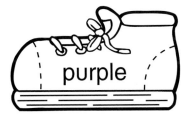 purple

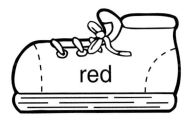 red

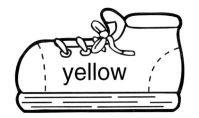 yellow

orange

purple

green

blue

yellow

red

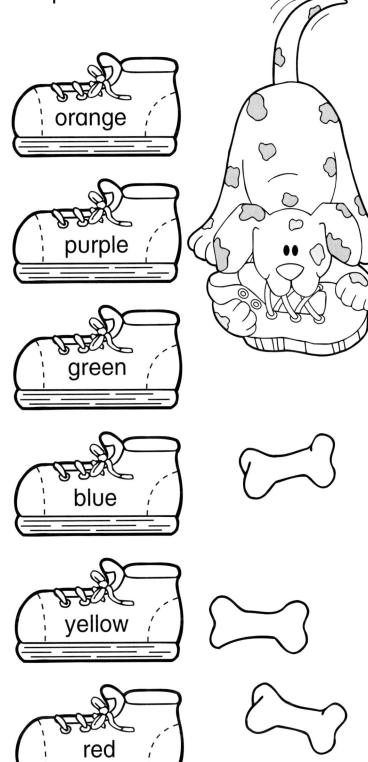

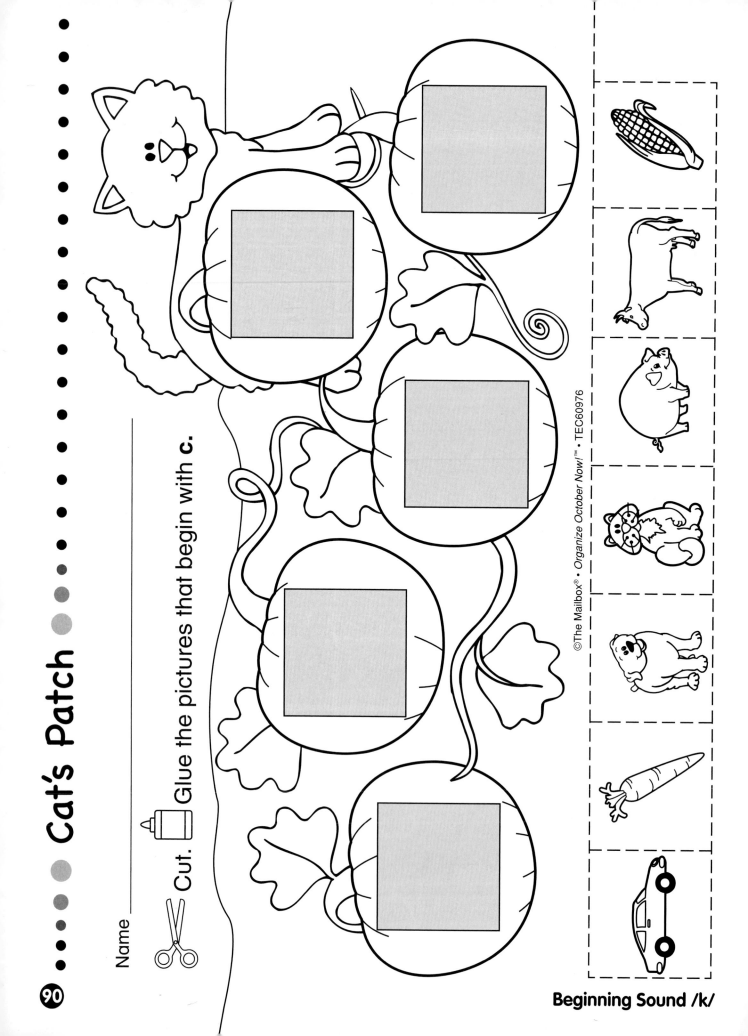

Cat's Patch

Name _____

✂ Cut. 🧴 Glue the pictures that begin with **c**.

90

©The Mailbox® • *Organize October Now!*™ • TEC60976

Beginning Sound /k/

Monster's Munchies

Name _____

Read the color words.

Color.

red

green

orange

brown

blue

yellow

purple

black

Squirreling Away Sounds

Name _____

✏️ Color to match beginning sounds.

Initial Consonants: b, m, s, w

A New Crop

Name _____

✂ Cut. 🖊 Glue to match beginning sounds.

ch			
sh			
th			

Digraphs: ch, sh, th 93

Spider's Pals

Name _____

🖍️ Color the set that shows less.

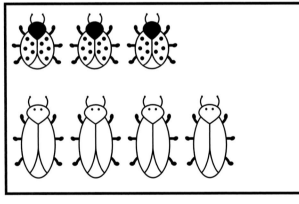

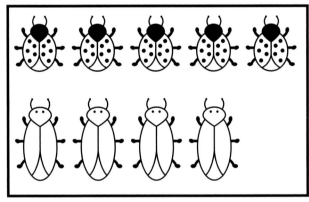

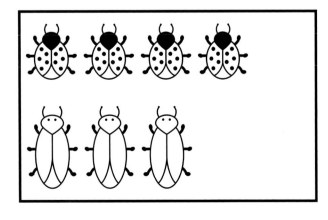

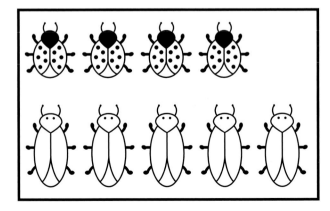

The Pick of the Patch

Name _____

Cut.

Glue to match shapes.

©The Mailbox® • *Organize October Now!*™ • TEC60976

Sweet Treats

Name _____

Subtract.

 out the candy corn to help you.

A.

5 – 3 = _____

B.

4 – 1 = _____

C.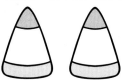

4 – 3 = _____

D.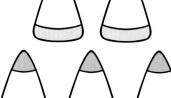

5 – 2 = _____

E.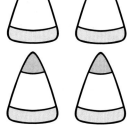

4 – 4 = _____

F.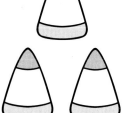

3 – 1 = _____

G.

5 – 1 = _____

H.

5 – 4 = _____